Tudor Exploration

Haydn Middleton

Heinemann

www.heinemann.co.uk/library
Visit our website to find out more information about **Heinemann Library** books.

To order:
 Phone 44 (0) 1865 888066
 Send a fax to 44 (0) 1865 314091
 Visit the Heinemann Bookshop at www.heinemann.co.uk/library to browse our catalogue and order online.

First published in Great Britain by Heinemann Library, Halley Court, Jordan Hill, Oxford OX2 8EJ, part of Harcourt Education.

Heinemann is a registered trademark of Harcourt Education Ltd.

Editorial: Lucy Thunder and Helen Cox
Design: Jo Hinton-Malivoire, Richard Parker and Tinstar Design Limited (www.tinstar.co.uk)
Illustrations: Tokay Interactive Ltd
Picture Research: Rebecca Sodergren
Production: Séverine Ribierre

Originated by Ambassador Litho Ltd
Printed and bound in China by
Leo Paper Productss Ltd.

ISBN 978 0 431 14618 8 (hardback)
07 06 05 04 03
10 9 8 7 6 5 4 3 2 1

ISBN 978 0431 14628 7 (paperback)
09
10 9 8 7 6 5

British Library Cataloguing in Publication Data
Middleton, Haydn
   Tudor exploration. – (People in the past)
   910.9'42'09031
A full catalogue record for this book is available from the British Library.

Acknowledgements
The publishers would like to thank the following for permission to reproduce photographs:

Bridgeman Art Archive/Bristol Museum p**22**; Bridgeman Art Archive p**36**; British Library Picture Library pp**14**, **15**, **26**, **28a**, **28b**, **31**, **34**, **40**; British Museum p**39**; Corbis p**38**; Fotomas Index pp**6**, **7**; Mary Evans Picture Library p**16**, **21**; National Maritime Museum pp**10**, **19**, **24**, **32**, **43**; National Portrait Gallery, p**30**; Ossie Palmer p**9**; Pepys Library pp**12**, **13**; Penguin/The Royal Collection 2003/Her Majesty Queen Elizabeth II p**42**

Cover photograph of ships off a rocky coast, 1540, reproduced with permission of The National Maritime Museum Picture Library.

The publishers would like to thank Rebecca Vickers for her assistance with the preparation of this book.

Contents

Words appearing in the text in bold, **like this**, are explained in the Glossary.

The Tudor world

How many continents are there? People today give different answers. Some say five: Europe, Asia, Africa, America and Australia. Some add Antarctica and say six. Others split South America from North America and say seven. Today we can look at maps of the world and decide. It was not like that over 500 years ago.

People then were not so well informed. Thanks to **trading** contacts, some Europeans knew that Asia and Africa existed. Yet even the most educated Europeans had no idea about America or Australia. People often relied on maps drawn over 1000 years before. Some people believed that the earth was flat!

This map gives a rough idea of the size of the world's **population** in early Tudor times. There were far more people living in Europe and Asia than in the rest of the world, and hardly any in America. Europe was split into different countries, some of which are shown here.

Then, in around 1500, things began to change. European sailors started to explore oceans and lands that were new to the people of Europe. They sailed around Africa to India, and across the Atlantic to America. Sometimes they traded in a friendly way with the people they met. Sometimes they fought, then turned these foreign lands into **colonies**. In this book, you can find out how and why explorers from England got involved.

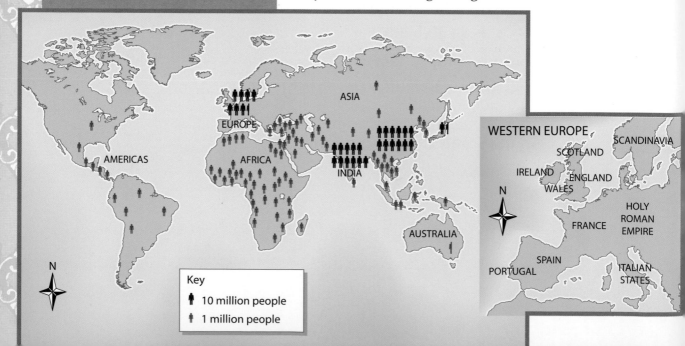

ASIA
EUROPE
AMERICAS
AFRICA
INDIA
AUSTRALIA

WESTERN EUROPE
SCANDINAVIA
SCOTLAND
IRELAND
ENGLAND
WALES
N
HOLY
ROMAN
EMPIRE
FRANCE
SPAIN
PORTUGAL
ITALIAN
STATES

Key
10 million people
1 million people

The Tudor family

The Tudor family ruled England and Wales from 1485 until 1603:
King Henry VII (king from 1485 to 1509)
King Henry VIII (king from 1509 to 1547)
King Edward VI (king from 1547 to 1553)
Queen Mary I (queen from 1553 to 1558)
Queen Elizabeth I (queen from 1558 to 1603)

Who were the Tudors?

Five hundred years ago Britain was very different too. England and Scotland were small, separate kingdoms, each with its own royal family. From 1485 to 1603 the Tudor family ruled over England, including the Principality of Wales. We now call this period 'Tudor times', and we know those who lived then as 'Tudor people'.

Most Tudor people lived in country villages, not in towns or big Tudor cities like London, Bristol or Norwich. The vast majority did farm work or made cloth in their own homes. Fishermen and traders did go out to sea, but they very rarely went far from the English coasts. And almost everyone believed in Christianity.

The brave and skilful Tudor explorers who sailed out into the unknown prayed hard to their God for protection. It is easy to see why. Today it seems amazing that they dared to cross vast oceans in such small wooden ships. By doing so, they helped to bring almost all the world's peoples into contact with one another.

Tudor money note

In this book, Tudor sums of money are shown in pounds (£), shillings (s) and pennies (d). There were 12d in a shilling and 20s in a pound – which was worth a lot more then! Most people earned less than £10 in a whole year, and you could go to the theatre for a single penny.

Dividing up the world

On the night of 20 May 1498, a sailing ship from Portugal dropped her anchor near the south-west coast of India. One of the sailors later wrote what happened next:

'Four [Indian] boats approached us from the land. They asked what nation we were. We told them … On the following day these boats came alongside again and took one of our men to the nearby city of Calicut … The first greeting he received was: 'May the devil take you! What brought you here?' They asked what we wanted, so far from home. We told him that we came in search of Christians and spices'.

Off to the Indies

European sailors did not go exploring just for fun. They wanted to learn of new lands in Asia – which they called 'the Indies'. Then **merchants** from their own countries could get rich by buying and selling goods there. They also wanted to find new routes to lands they already knew about, like China. The Italian sea-captain Christopher Columbus (1451–1506), for example, tried to travel westwards to reach the Indies. That was when he unexpectedly found the West Indies in his way, and – beyond them – America.

A Tudor map of Africa. Many Europeans believed that either here or in Asia there was a Christian ruler called 'Prester John'. One of the explorers' aims was to track him down. They never found him.

This scene shows a pepper-growing district in southern India. Pepper was one of several **spices** – like cinnamon, ginger and cloves – desired by Europeans. Spices helped to liven up rich people's food and drink, and were also used as dyes, drugs and perfumes. It was cheaper to bring them to Europe by sea, than by long routes overland through Asia.

Some European **monarchs** paid for voyages of exploration. The first were the rulers of Portugal and Spain. To stop them from competing overseas, they signed the **Treaty** of Tordesillas in 1494. With the blessing of the mighty **Catholic Pope** in Rome, they drew a line on a map of the world. Then they agreed that any lands discovered to the west of it would go to Spain, any to the east would go to Portugal. Other European countries were not supposed to send out their own explorers. Soon, however, France did, and so did Tudor England …

First impressions of the Indians of the West

Christopher Columbus was Italian, but the monarchs of Spain paid him to explore for them. Seeking a western route to the Asian Indies, he reached the Caribbean Islands in 1492. He reported back on the 'Indians' he found there (later known as 'American Indians' or 'Amerindians'): 'They are very well made, with very handsome bodies and very good faces …
They should be good servants and intelligent. They quickly took in what was said to them, and I believe that they would easily be made Christians.'

The English overseas

How interested were Tudor English people in exploring overseas?
Lots of them knew nothing about it. (There were no newspapers
to describe the achievements of Christopher Columbus and other
foreign captains. Besides, most ordinary people could not read!)
Unless you were rich, it was unusual to make long journeys inside
England, let alone abroad. One group of people did have an
interest in the outside world – **merchants** who lived by **trading**.

Europe and the wider world

In early Tudor times, lots of goods were shipped in and out of
England. From abroad came luxury goods like fine French wines
and **spices**, silks and precious stones from the Indies, plus
important raw materials like iron. England's main **export** was
cloth made from wool.

By 1550 more English woollen cloth was being sold abroad than
ever before, and for very good prices. This made many merchants
rich. It also helped the **monarchs** of England: they got merchants
to pay a **tax** called 'customs duty' on many traded goods. In times
of warfare they also made use of merchants' ships for fighting.

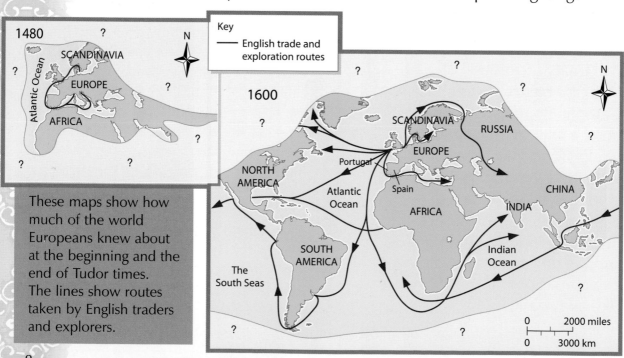

Key
— English trade and exploration routes

1480

1600

These maps show how
much of the world
Europeans knew about
at the beginning and the
end of Tudor times.
The lines show routes
taken by English traders
and explorers.

Much of England's foreign trade was based in Antwerp. Antwerp, in the country we now call Belgium, was a huge trading centre just across the English Channel. Cloth was shipped there from London. Then foreign merchants took it on to places as far away as Turkey and Persia. Large amounts of luxury goods from distant lands also came to London via Antwerp.

During Tudor times, England's monarchs stayed more interested in Europe than in other continents. However, rich **courtiers**, merchants and gentlemen tried to make sure England was not left behind in the race to find new lands and opportunities overseas (see box above). In this book you can find out about the main voyages they paid for. And, on the next two pages, you will also find that events in Europe could have a big effect on Tudor overseas exploration.

This Tudor trading ship dates from 1517. Merchant John Greneway had it carved on the wall of his own chapel at St Peter's church, Tiverton.

Christians in conflict

'Different men give different reasons for the discoveries [of new countries]. Some want power, and new places to rule over. Others seek worldly gain, often by dishonest and unlawful means. Fewest of all talk of the glory of God, and saving the souls of poor **infidels**.'

So wrote the Tudor English priest and author Richard Hakluyt (c.1553–1616, pronounced 'Hak-let').

Many early Tudor explorers *did* however believe they were serving God. Later explorers aimed not just to make foreign peoples Christians. They also wanted to save foreigners from the 'wrong' sort of Christianity. For English explorers that meant spreading the **Protestant** version of the faith, not the **Catholic** one. By the end of Tudor times, England had become Europe's leading Protestant nation, while Spain was the main Catholic power. This meant that they clashed, both in Europe and beyond.

Even so, from early to mid-Tudor times, England was on good terms with Spain. King Henry VIII's first and longest-lasting wife was the Spanish princess, Catherine of Aragon. Then their daughter, Queen Mary I, married King Philip II of Spain.

In 1588 Philip II of Spain sent out a mighty fleet of ships or 'Armada' to land an invading army in England. English pirate-captains Francis Drake and John Hawkins played a major part in organizing the successful defence of England's shores.

Religious refuges overseas

The English were not very successful at making the Native American peoples Christian, but there were plans to send English people with strong religious beliefs to set up **colonies** there. Some English people continued to worship as Catholics under Elizabeth I and they were **fined** for this. Sir Thomas Gerard, who was Catholic, gave money to support a scheme to send Catholics to America. Then, in the 1590s, some extreme Protestants called **Puritans** planned to start a truly 'godly' colony there. It was not until after Tudor times, however, that successful English Catholic and Puritan colonies were set up – in Maryland and New England.

Philip II ruled Spain from 1556 to 1598. As well as his Spanish kingdom, he ruled over an **empire** that included parts of Italy, the **Low Countries** (where Antwerp was), and – after 1580 – Portugal. It also included massive areas of South and Central America – regions 'discovered' by Spanish explorers, then **conquered** by Spanish soldiers and **colonized** by Spanish **settlers**.

England and Spain drift apart

By the **Treaty** of Tordesillas (see page 7), Europeans from other countries – including England – were not meant to interfere in the Spanish empire, or go exploring across the Atlantic. But, after Queen Mary died in 1558, her half-sister Elizabeth became queen. Under her rule, England became, and stayed, a Protestant country. From 1585 until 1604 England was at war with Spain.

During that time, English seamen felt more free to do as they liked overseas. They explored in north and south America, and they traded with Spain and Portugal's hugely wealthy colonies. They even became pirates, robbed enemy ships, and brought treasure back to Europe across the Atlantic Ocean. Often they used the same ships to carry out all these activities!

The ships the Tudors sailed in

Today little survives of the wooden sailing ships used by Tudor explorers. For information about them, we have to rely on pictures from the time, and from written descriptions. In about 1586, a Tudor **shipwright** called Matthew Baker wrote: 'the width of a ship is a matter of personal choice. The length must never be less than double the width, nor more than treble it.'

Ocean-going vessels

Early Tudor ships did not need to make long voyages. Many sailed only the short distance to Antwerp and back. These trips could be made overnight in good weather. The ships were not suitable for long ocean expeditions that might involve fighting as well as **trading**. So in later Tudor times ships were designed to be stronger, easier to steer and with enough weapons to make them fearsome. (Tudor England was famous for its brass cannons.)

The ships were built with **timbers** of English oak, elm and pine. They had three or four fir masts, carrying both square and triangular sails. Main masts could be 18 metres tall. That meant cutting down healthy trees with no branches or flaws for their first 18 metres.

Shipwrights designed ships in which the captain and officers had 'quarters' (small rooms) to the ship's 'stern' or rear. The ordinary sailors had to squeeze together on the gun deck when not on duty. Here, Matthew Baker is shown working with dividers.

This ocean-going vessel, the *Jesus of Lubeck*, was part of the Royal Navy under Elizabeth I. Such ships had to be well 'caulked' to make them watertight. This meant wedging unravelled ropes between the ship's planks. The ropes were then covered with hot melted pitch (tar).

In the thick forests of Tudor England there were many more such trees around than today. But even these new, improved ships would have looked cramped and flimsy to us.

Francis Drake took a ship only 23 metres long around the world between 1577 and 1580, with up to 80 men on board. Plenty of things could go wrong on a voyage. Bad weather or enemy cannon shots could cause violent leaks. **Rudders** or anchors were easily lost and masts damaged. Ice and fog in some regions were extremely dangerous, and storms were the single worst cause of disaster.

Different types of Tudor ship

The biggest ocean-going ships, used for battle and carrying **cargo**, were called galleons. They had at least three decks and three masts. Smaller, lighter ships, called caravels, were often used for exploration, since they were easier to steer. Many large ships carried 'pinnaces' below decks. These were small boats used for exploring coastlines, sending out messengers, or boarding other ships. There were also 'galliasses', that could be moved along by oars as well as sails. Sometimes oarsmen rowed **barges** filled with soldiers alongside bigger ships to protect them.

'A nation of pirates'

By late-Tudor times, foreign writers often called the English 'a nation of pirates'. This was because Queen Elizabeth I let the crews of privately owned ships attack enemy ships and seize their goods in wartime. This was called **privateering**. The **privateers** often seized **neutral** ships and goods too. Then they sold their 'prizes' in distant ports and shared out the money they made.

Giovanni Scaramelli, a visitor to London from Venice in 1603, wrote this: 'The English, through their greed and cruelty, have become hateful to all nations. They are at open war with Spain and are already robbing her and her trading ships; they are continually robbing the French with violence … They are disturbers of the whole world.'

Discipline problems

Many Tudor seamen signed up for long voyages hoping to make a fortune. Around 1000 Spanish and Portuguese ships were captured between 1585 and 1603. Attracted by that, some men did not even ask to be paid (usually up to £1 a month), and were ready to put up with 'a hard cabin, cold and salty meat, broken sleep, mouldy bread, flat beer, wet clothes, and lack of fire,' as Luke Fox, an **Arctic** explorer from Hull, said.

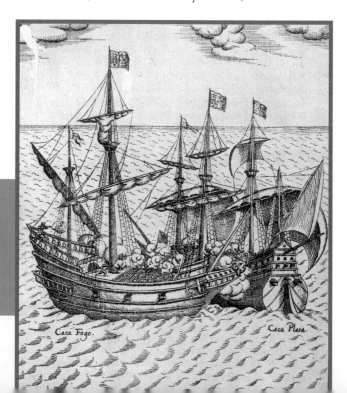

An English vessel (right) about to seize a Spanish ship off the west coast of South America in 1579. The cargo of silver bars, gold and coin was worth about £150,000 today. In Tudor times that was a massive sum.

Skilled sailors

Some Tudor seamen trained as **apprentices** for lifelong careers at sea. Many became ship's masters, often owning or part-owning the vessels they sailed in. Masters could earn £5 or £6 a month, plus more from trading or carrying goods for **merchants**. Thanks to the many dangers of seafaring, however, there was a shortage of skilled sailors. 'Few live to grow grey hairs,' wrote Richard Hakluyt, who tried and failed to start up a national training scheme for seamen.

Men like these could be hard to control at sea. 'Crews,' wrote Sir Richard Hawkins, 'are like a stiff-necked horse that gets the bridle between its teeth, and forces the rider [or captain] to go wherever it wishes.' There were often fights in the cramped conditions. Captains tried to keep order with harsh punishments. If a crew rose up in **mutiny**, however, there was little a captain could do. In 1611, for example, the explorer Henry Hudson found this out the hard way. After his crew mutinied he was set adrift by his men and left to die off North America.

The Spanish **conquered** much of South and Central America and the West Indies. By 1575, about 69,000 European **colonists** lived in the 'New World'. Many grew rich by using African slaves like these to mine gold and silver, and grow sugar from canes.

Surviving at sea

Life at sea was full of dangers and difficulties. In April 1585 a ship named the *Tiger* left Plymouth under its captain Sir Richard Grenville. It headed for America, where those on board hoped to start a **colony**. Despite a bad storm, it reached the Caribbean Sea in just 21 days. It was so hot there that several sailors took a dip in the surf to cool off. A shark bit off the leg of one sailor. The sailor's stump was dipped in a vat of boiling pitch (tar) to seal it up. By then, the ship's biscuits were full of beetles, the dried cheese had gone bad, and there were so many worms in the water, the sailors had to clench their teeth when they drank it to stop swallowing them. Finally, when the ship reached its destination, another storm almost broke it apart.

Food, fever and fighting

Accidents on board often happened carrying out daily duties. The food supply had to last for the whole voyage, or until seamen could get ashore at any islands on route to top it up. Without fridges, fresh food did not keep. For long periods sailors made do with dried and salted meat or fish.

An Italian picture of a Tudor sailor, from 1598. In Tudor times there were no sailors' uniforms, and no armour to protect them during sea battles.

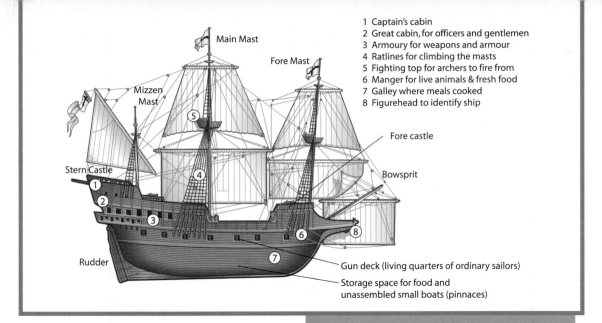

1 Captain's cabin
2 Great cabin, for officers and gentlemen
3 Armoury for weapons and armour
4 Ratlines for climbing the masts
5 Fighting top for archers to fire from
6 Manger for live animals & fresh food
7 Galley where meals cooked
8 Figurehead to identify ship

Main Mast
Fore Mast
Mizzen Mast
Fore castle
Stern Castle
Bowsprit
Rudder
Gun deck (living quarters of ordinary sailors)
Storage space for food and unassembled small boats (pinnaces)

They would eat this with ship's biscuits or 'hardtack' made from flour and water, and liquids that included water, vinegar, wine, beer and port.

Lack of fresh fruit or vegetables meant that many sailors were struck down by a disease called **scurvy**. We now know this disease was caused by a lack of vitamin C. 'My thighs and lower legs were black,' wrote a victim. 'I had to use my knife each day to cut into the flesh, to release the black and foul blood.' **Fevers** spread fast in the rat-infested, dirty conditions.

There were further dangers when enemy ships attacked. Seamen then had to work the cannons – or use guns, swords, spears, clubs, bows and arrows for closer fighting. Yet the excitement of battle may have been welcome after weeks of hunger, illness or boredom.

A typical medium-sized ocean-going ship. There was not much headroom on the lower decks, like the gun-deck where ordinary sailors slept. However, the average man's height in later Tudor times was only about 163 centimetres.

What Tudor sailors wore

'Their clothes are made of wool,' wrote an Italian observer in 1598, 'and are yellowish-red and white. Their cloaks are short, their **breeches** longish, wide, baggy and full of folds. Their hats are shaggy and made of felt.' Few Tudor sailors would have taken more than one outfit on a voyage – and hardly any of these have survived. In 1545 an English ship, the *Mary Rose*, sank at Portsmouth. Deep mud stopped some leather shoes and jackets on the sailors' skeletons from rotting. In the late 20th century divers went down and brought them up to the surface. You can see them today in a museum in Portsmouth.

Sailors' information

Tudor seamen often sailed where few Europeans had sailed before. On such voyages, they had little idea what they would find. So they gathered information from wherever they could.

Some information came from other sailors' stories. These could, however, be misleading. One story told of a region in the far north called 'Thule'. It was said to be neither land nor sea nor air, but a weird mixture of all three! Sailors also heard tales about beasts and monsters that lived in the oceans. A dead one – a 'sea unicorn' – was actually found by the explorer Martin Frobisher (see page 26). In fact it was a 'narwhal', a member of the whale and dolphin family. Captain Frobisher still presented the 'unicorn's' horn as a gift to Queen Elizabeth I!

Useful tools

Tudor sailors got information in scientific ways too. To measure the depth of the sea, for example, they used a long **cable** hung with lead weights. And although there were no clocks at sea, they could keep time with a 'sandglass' (like an egg timer). They also tried to work out where they were by checking the positions of the sun and well-known stars. Tools called 'astrolabes' and 'cross-staffs' let them work out how far north or south they were.

Messages in the stars

Before sailing into the unknown, many **superstitious** seamen studied **horoscopes**, written by **astrologers**, for information. In 1585 the astrologer Thomas Porter wrote this warning: 'If any man has journeys to take by land or by water, let him keep his wits about him, for force is likely to be strong in all places, and violence already shakes its head and frowns at travellers … Caution and courage are the best spells against such sprites and goblins.' However, since he also said that plague and **fevers** were about to strike in cities and towns at home, it was probably not a good idea to postpone the voyage!

A compass from the 1500s. It worked by using the magnet inside to point to the north, thus helping sailors to find their way. It was not very accurate.

Knots and logs

To work out a ship's speed, sailors used their sandglass and a 'log-line'. This was a piece of wood with a rope wound round it. The rope had a weight attached to its end. You threw the weight overboard, then watched the rope unravel. Knots had been tied in it, at equal distances apart. You counted how many knots appeared during the time it took for the sand to run through the sandglass. Then you were able to say that the ship was travelling at a speed of three or four or five 'knots'. Ship speeds today are still measured in knots.

The English sail to America

In 1497, Tudor sailors made one of their first great voyages of exploration – to the mainland of North America. They may have been the first Europeans ever to set foot there, but they did not know they had reached America.

They had set out from England – 35 days before – hoping to sail westwards to Asia. King Henry VII had given them his permission to take control of any new lands they found, and to **trade** with any peoples they met. Like the crew of Christopher Columbus five years earlier, the English seamen had not realized that the continent of America would block their route. So they thought they had got to Asia!

The first great Tudor explorer

The captain of the English ship, the *Matthew*, was not English. He was an Italian called Giovanni Caboto (c.1455–98) – known in England as John Cabot. Like Columbus, he worked for whichever European **monarch** would pay him to go exploring.

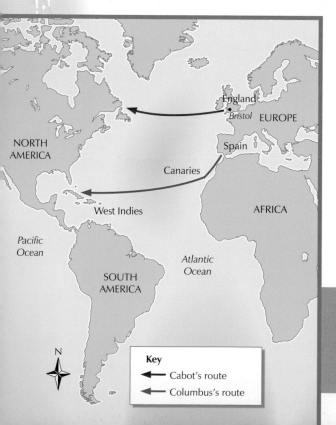

Key
← Cabot's route
← Columbus's route

In a letter of 1497, an Italian **ambassador** in London described what Cabot did for Henry VII: 'He set sail in a little ship, with eighteen persons on board. He started from Bristol, a port on the west of this kingdom, passed Ireland … and then headed towards the north … After wandering for some time he at last arrived at the mainland. There he hoisted the royal flag, in King Henry's name.'

Cabot's route across the Atlantic was shorter and quicker than Columbus's. Cabot brought back no treasure but Henry VII was so pleased that he rewarded him with a payment of £20 a year.

Where did Cabot land in America?

Since we do not know exactly what route Cabot took in 1497, we cannot be sure where he landed in north-east America. Some historians believe he reached the shore of Nova Scotia in the country we now call Canada. Others think it was the Labrador coast. The most likely place was Newfoundland, a large island near the modern Canadian coast, at the mouth of the St. Lawrence River. Tudor people certainly talked about a 'new found land' across the ocean – but that could have meant any part of north-east America.

The explorers stayed in America for only a short time, and made no contact with any people.

It must have been disappointing to find no wealthy cities, and no gold or **spices** to take back to England. The explorers thought they had simply landed in the wrong part of Asia. In 1498, Cabot was captain on another voyage west, this time with five ships. His aim was to find 'Cipangu' or Japan, where he believed many spices were grown. One ship turned back after storm damage. The others, including Cabot, sailed on but were never heard from again.

Even before 1497, Bristol fishermen sailed far out into the Atlantic looking for good fishing-grounds. Cabot's crew believed – quite rightly – that huge amounts of cod could be caught off the new-found coast of America.

Sailing north to Asia

King Henry VII kept up his interest in westward exploration. In 1502 he gave £20 to 'the **merchants** of Bristol that have been in the new found land'. Three men from there – either Native Americans or **Inuits** – were brought back to his court. Later 'presents' from trading voyages included a bow and arrows, mountain cats and parrots.

As it became clear that America was not Asia, some explorers aimed to sail above the 'new' land mass and so reach Asia. They dreamed of finding a 'north-west passage' to the East. Sadly for them, King Henry VIII, who ruled from 1509 to 1547, was not so keen on overseas exploration. He preferred to focus on Europe – waging war against England's old enemy, France. For this he needed the support of England's old **ally**, Spain. So he did not want to upset the Spanish by sending ships to regions that, according to the 1494 **Treaty** of Tordesillas, 'belonged' to them (see page 7). Besides, the explorers' schemes could sound odd ...

Sebastian Cabot (1476–1557) may have sailed with his father John to North America in 1497. He then served several European **monarchs** as an explorer and mapmaker. He was also successful as a merchant and businessman.

Like father, like son

Richard Hakluyt included in his book *Principal Navigations* (see page 42) these words from Sebastian Cabot: 'All men declared it would be a truly wonderful thing to sail westward by a new route into the East, where **spices** grow. As this talk went around, there rose in my heart a burning desire to find such a route. By looking at the globe, I realised that if I sailed in a north-westerly direction, I should by a shorter journey come to India.' Sebastian, like his father John, would spend much time and energy searching for the north-west passage to Asia.

The Bristol merchant Robert Thorne wanted to voyage over the North Pole into the Pacific Ocean, leaving North America on the left. Another scheme – Richard Hore's 1536 expedition to Newfoundland – got some support from Henry VIII but ended badly. The main ship ran short of food near Newfoundland and the men on board began eating one another. Finally they seized a French ship with its stores and sailed home. That ended the interest of King Henry and any other **backers** who might support such voyages.

Time for a change

Until the 1550s, most of London's wealthiest merchants concentrated on trading with Antwerp. They ignored other overseas trade. As members of a trading company – the Merchant Adventurers – they were used to making huge **profits** from this link. But then, as there was so much cloth around, its price at Antwerp began to fall. This made some merchants consider branching out.

Under the new Tudor king, Edward VI, who ruled from 1547 to 1553, John Cabot's son Sebastian got a top job with the Merchant Adventurers. His special aim was to 'discover regions, islands and places unknown.' With Sebastian in charge, seamen set out to find new routes to places where English woollen cloth might be sold. An early success came when one expedition arrived, by chance, in Russia …

Reaching Russia

In May 1553 two ships containing 116 men left London. Sebastian Cabot had helped to persuade 200 **backers** to pay £6000 for this 'new and strange' voyage. The soldier Sir Hugh Willoughby and the **navigator** Richard Chancellor led the expedition. Its aim was to sail north-eastwards, passing above Scandinavia and Russia (then called Muscovy), and find an ice-free route to 'the Indies'. English **merchants** might then sell their woollen cloth there – and in other lands along the way. Sebastian Cabot gave strict instructions on how the seamen should treat any new customers they met. 'Every nation is to be respected,' he wrote. 'They must not be laughed at.'

Major trading breakthrough

In September Sir Hugh Willoughby's ship lost its way. Its 70-man crew could not survive the bitter **Arctic** winter, which included five weeks of non-stop night. Their frozen bodies were found the next summer.

Richard Chancellor's ship found no northern route to the East either. Instead it sailed into the White Sea and landed in Russia. He used 'signs and gestures' to talk with the local people. He then travelled overland for 2400 kilometres (1500 miles), often by sledge, to Moscow – a city 'as great as London'.

No Tudor expedition managed to find a north-eastern passage to the Indies. This picture shows an equally unsuccessful Dutch attempt. In terribly cold weather, the sailors had to try to clear ice from the ship's path, while keeping an eye out for angry polar bears.

The routes taken by Richard Chancellor in 1553 and Anthony Jenkinson in 1557.

He was welcomed by the Russian 'tsar' or ruler, Ivan IV. Ivan eagerly agreed to start trading with English merchants – he was especially keen to buy English cannon. Within a few years, English merchants were shipping woollens and other goods in bulk to Russia. In return came Russian items like furs, hides, **flax**, and rope that was used for ships' **cables**. These merchants belonged to the new Muscovy Company in London. The company organized all the **trading** – and also sent out explorers to find other useful trade routes (see box).

Richard Chancellor himself was drowned on a voyage back from Russia in 1556. But, by opening up trade with this distant land, he had made a major Tudor breakthrough in finding overseas customers.

Jenkinson's journeys

In 1557 the Muscovy Company sent a gentleman called Anthony Jenkinson to Russia. His mission was to find a route through Russia into central Asia, where new trade links could be made. He travelled on foot from Moscow to Bokhara, where he found the merchants too 'beggarly and poor' to make any **trade** worthwhile. In 1561 he made another journey, this time arriving at the court of the Shah of Persia. The Muslim Shah had little time for him, declaring: 'We have no need for friendship with **infidels**.' Jenkinson's journeys helped atlas-makers – like the great Abraham Ortelius (1527–1598) of Antwerp – to draw more accurate maps of these little-known regions.

The north-west project

In June 1576 the Muscovy (Russia) Company made an attempt to find a north-west passage to Asia. It sent out a small expedition captained by Martin Frobisher (c.1535–1594), who had been a sailor since the age of fourteen. They set sail across the Atlantic, and after passing Greenland, the ships came to the southern tip of Baffin Island, which is today a part of Canada.

Martin Frobisher found a bay or **strait**, which he hoped to sail through and so reach the Indies. Despite it being the month of August, everything was frozen. Frobisher could not continue his voyage. He turned back to England, but was determined to return and try again.

Inuits in England

These words come from *Adams's Chronicle of Bristol*, published in 1623: 'In 1577 Captain Frobisher brought to England a man called Callicho, and a woman called Ignorth … On 9 October Callicho rowed in a little boat made of skin in the water at the quay. There he killed two ducks with a dart, and when he had finished, he carried his boat through the marsh upon his back. He did the same at the weir, and at other places where many watched him.' Sadly the Inuits could not cope with England's different climate, and soon they both died.

Frobisher's findings

Martin Frobisher led two more expeditions to the Canadian coast, in 1577 and 1578. He did not find a north-western passage. The Tudor historian William Camden wrote, 'tossed up and down by the foul weather, snows and changing winds, [Frobisher] gathered a great quantity of stones.' Frobisher hoped gold or silver might be found inside them. This did not turn out to be true and the stones were used instead to mend roads!

Captain Frobisher's three voyages sound like failures. Yet as a result of his explorations, maps of northern America could be drawn more accurately. He also made many Europeans interested in the native people there – the **Inuits** (once known as Eskimos).

Inuits

The Inuits seized and possibly killed five of Captain Frobisher's men when they first met, but he found them fascinating. He wanted to bring some Inuit children back to England, 'educate' them and turn them into Christians. In fact he brought two adults (see box). On his third voyage, he left behind for the Inuits a little house built of lime and stone. Inside it he put bells, knives, pictures, mirrors and an oven with baked bread. He hoped this would lead them to live more like the English.

Like many Tudor explorers, Martin Frobisher believed everyone should copy English ways. Today we believe it is more helpful to respect the ways that other people have chosen to live.

A picture from around 1580 showing the Inuits seen by Frobisher. Here they are hunting seabirds; on the shore is a summer camp of sealskin tents. Since the real Inuits looked a little like Chinese or Mongolian people, the English explorers thought they must be near East Asia.

New maps, new plans

Tudor **merchants** and explorers kept searching for a north-west passage. After Martin Frobisher, a fine **navigator** called John Davis tried his luck. Davis led three expeditions into the **Arctic** from 1585 to 1587, and found the mouth of the Hudson **Strait** that leads deep into Canada. Although he never learned if he could reach the East by travelling down it, his explorations added greatly to European knowledge of northern America. (His men also played football with **Inuits**, thus adding to *their* knowledge of sport!)

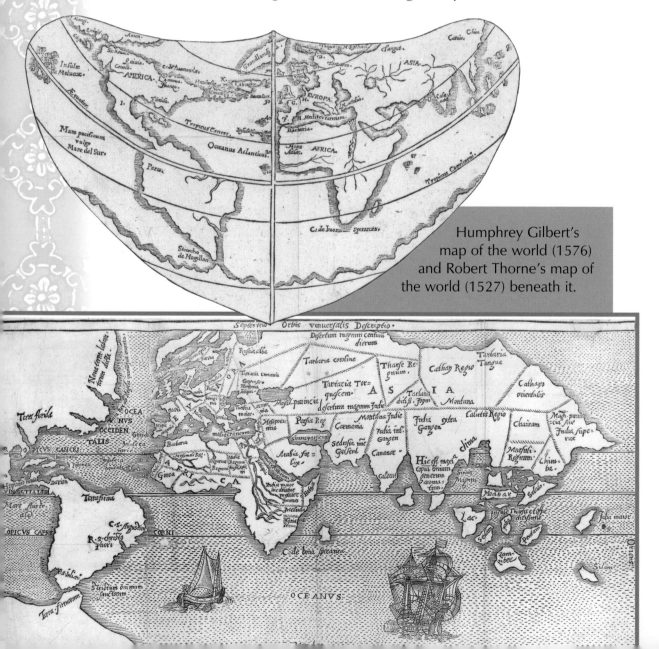

Humphrey Gilbert's map of the world (1576) and Robert Thorne's map of the world (1527) beneath it.

Filling in the details

The Devonshire gentleman and soldier Humphrey Gilbert was another firm believer in the north-west passage to Asia. He wrote a book about it, and drew his own world map. You can see a version, from 1576, on page 28. Below it is an earlier map, drawn by the English merchant Robert Thorne. This dates from 1527, shortly after a Spanish crew completed the first ever voyage right around the world (1519–1522).

Robert Thorne believed 'every sea can be sailed, every land can be lived in'. His map (see page 28) showed no possibility of a north-east or north-west passage to the Indies. Humphrey Gilbert's map from 50 years later showed the world's coastlines in much greater detail. Yet still he showed a non-existent passage to the East above North America. Wishful thinking!

In 1583 Humphrey Gilbert turned to a new project. He took about 260 men across to North American Newfoundland. He wanted them to make lasting homes for themselves there, while still being ruled from England. A community like this was called a **colony**. The project was not supported by Elizabeth I, and it failed. But, the plan to 'plant' English people in America would live on in Tudor minds.

Creatures for man to 'use'

Edward Haye was a survivor of Humphrey Gilbert's colony. He later wrote: 'We found many sorts of hawks, plentiful partridges larger than ours, grey and white and rough-footed like doves. Our men killed them with **cudgels**, since they were so fat and unable to fly … There were animals of many kinds – red deer, buffaloes … Also bears, leopards, wolves, black-furred foxes.' Edward Haye said the **colonists** thanked God for filling that distant land with so many creatures, just for them to 'use' in various ways.

Drake sets sail

'His name was a terror to the French, Spaniard, Portuguese and Indians. Many princes of Italy, Germany and elsewhere wanted his picture during his lifetime, enemies as well as friends.' Who was this great Tudor 'sea-dog', described here by historian Edmund Howes in his *Chronicles* (1615)? It was Sir Francis Drake. He first became famous as a **privateer**, attacking the ships of other European countries. Then in 1580 he became the first English captain to sail around the world.

Francis Drake (c.1543–96). According to Edmund Howes he was: 'Short, with strong limbs, broad-chested, round-headed, brown hair, full-bearded, his eyes large, round and clear.'

Mystery trip

On 13 December 1577 Francis Drake left Plymouth in Devon, his own home county, with five well-armed ships. On board were around 20 officers and gentlemen, with a crew of 164 men – including a shoemaker, musicians, several ships' boys and a preacher. They sailed south, then headed across the Atlantic towards South America.

What was the purpose of their voyage? Most of those on board had not been told. Even today we cannot be sure what the secret plans were.

Francis Drake's **backers** – including several top **courtiers** and maybe even Queen Elizabeth I – expected him to seize some Spanish treasure. They probably also wanted him to discover new routes to the Indies, and open up some new **trade** for English goods. Maybe they even hoped he would find places to start English **colonies**.

Francis Drake soon captured some treasure, plus a Portuguese **pilot** – called Nuno da Silva – to help him **navigate** the eastern coasts of South America. The coasts proved so foggy and frightening that Drake started to think there was a male 'witch' on board who was poisoning the atmosphere. His suspicion fell on the gentleman Thomas Doughty, who also seemed to be poisoning the crews' minds against *him*. On 20 June 1578, Drake put him on trial for **mutiny**. Found guilty, Doughty was executed.

Now Drake had to lead his expedition around the bottom of South America – from the Atlantic Ocean into the Pacific. No English captain had ever navigated these treacherous waters before …

This book by John Dee (1577) called on men like Drake to set up colonies as part of the 'British Empire'.

Drake described by his enemies

Francis Drake forced Nuno da Silva to be his pilot, but the Portuguese sailor found him 'a great captain … He kept a book recording details of the voyage, with his own drawings of birds, trees and sea lions. He is a very good painter.' Captain Drake later presented this book to Queen Elizabeth I. Another prisoner, the Spaniard Don Francisco de Zarate, wrote that his crew treated Drake with respect, but he was always quick to punish their mistakes. He also liked to lead his men in prayers and **psalm** singing, since he was a keen **Protestant**.

31

Drake voyages on

Francis Drake passed successfully from the Atlantic Ocean into the Pacific. On the way, he claimed three small islands for Queen Elizabeth I. What he did *not* find underneath South America was a great southern continent – 'Terra Australis'.

Some Tudor people were sure such a continent was there. They thought it was just waiting to be discovered by the English. Richard Grenville wrote before Captain Drake set sail: 'Portugal has won one part of the new-found world in the east. Spain has taken another in the west, and France a third in the north. Now God has left the fourth part, in the south, for England.' Drake did not find it.

This instrument for **navigating** dates from 1569. It is called 'Drake's dial' and may possibly once have belonged to him. We know that he took on his voyage three books on navigation, one in French, and a Portuguese map of the world.

'The dragon' strikes

Francis Drake now headed up the west coast of South America. By autumn 1578 only one ship out of the whole fleet, the *Golden Hind*, was sailing on. Some men on the other ships transferred to the *Golden Hind*; some headed back home; some died in storms. The survivors led by Drake continued to attack a series of Spanish ports and ships. Their greatest prize was the captured treasure ship nicknamed *Cacafuego*. Its **cargo** of silver bars, gold and coin was worth the then massive sum of £140,000.

The Spanish – who were not officially at war with England – both feared and admired Drake. They called him *El Draque*, meaning 'The Dragon'. They believed he had superhuman powers – and a magic mirror to see where their ships were at sea. Spanish parents told naughty children that *El Draque* would get them if they did not behave!

The *Golden Hind* headed up the west coast of North America. Drake hoped to find the entrance to the north-west passage (see page 26), which would lead to a quick, eastward route home. He found no such passage. From 17 June to 23 July 1579 he stayed at a harbour in what is now called California. Then it was time to head *westward* for home, around the bottom of Africa.

New Albion

On 26 June 1579 Francis Drake was staying on the North American coast. The local Native American chief came up with a guard of about 100 men. Then, singing a song, he set a crown on Drake's head, put chains around his neck and offered him many gifts. Drake declared that since Spain had no **colony** on this land, it could now be ruled by Queen Elizabeth I and later **monarchs**. He called it 'New Albion' – Albion was an ancient name for England. Long after Drake's time, English **colonists** thought this gave them a 'right' to make their homes in North America.

Drake returns

Francis Drake now aimed to reach home as quickly and safely as possible. But, when the *Golden Hind* reached the Molucca Islands, east of India, he saw a chance to **trade** with the local people. For this was where many exotic **spices** came from. The ruler of one island, Ternate, was happy to do a deal with Drake, even though he was supposed to trade only with the Portuguese. Drake took aboard about six tons of **cloves**. No English captain had made such direct contact with people in this region before. (After Drake opened the way, an 'East India Company' was formed to organize the new trade.)

After 1580, many maps soon appeared showing the route of Francis Drake's 'Famous Voyage'. This is a French version, from around 1582–83. The round picture shows Drake at the age of 42. The little picture on the right shows the *Golden Hind* when it struck an East Indian reef and nearly sank in early 1580.

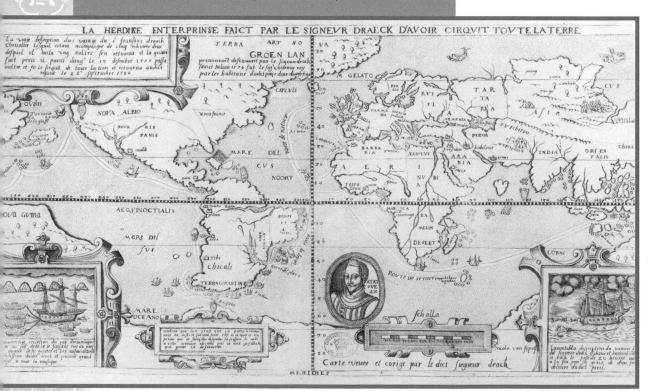

Seafood for sailors

Francis Drake's men gathered whatever food they could find locally. At different stages of the voyage, this included seals, penguins and sharks. At 'Crab Island' in the Indian Ocean, they caught, boiled and ate some big grass-eating crabs that lived in holes at the roots of trees. The scientist Charles de l'Ecluse talked to some crew members in 1581 and made notes on these strange creatures. Apparently they could be 60 centimetres wide, and one 'fed four hungry men at a dinner.'

On the night of 8–9 January 1580, disaster struck. Strong winds drove the ship off course amid a group of Indonesian islands. The *Golden Hind* hit a **reef** and stayed stuck until the next afternoon. Some sailors feared that this was God's punishment for all the **privateering**. The crew had to throw away three tons of cloves, two guns and some stores to lighten the ship and get it floating again. (They did not heave any of their captured treasure over the side!)

They then sailed south of Java – proving it was an island and not the tip of a great southern continent – passed by the Cape of Good Hope at the foot of Africa, and finally reached Plymouth on 26 September 1580.

'Master thief of the unknown world'

How would Elizabeth I now greet Francis Drake? The Spanish were pressing her to make him give back the treasure he had seized. The queen did not want to offend the King of Spain, so some of it was returned. Most of the treasure was kept, however – and she herself took an enormous share.

Unlike some less successful **privateers**, Drake was not put on trial. ('Only those who steal too little suffer,' joked one writer.) In fact the queen let him keep £10,000, with £10,000 more for his crew, and in April 1581 she made him a knight. Thrilled, she had listened for six hours as he told her the story of his voyage. As an explorer, and as a thief, no Tudor sea captain had ever achieved so much.

Raleigh's Roanoke project

Some Tudor writers wanted England to create a great overseas **empire** like Spain's. They gave several reasons for **colonies** to be set up. Firstly, a colony on the American coast could serve as a **naval** base for attacks on the wealthy Spanish empire. Secondly, English **colonists** could turn the local Native American peoples into 'civilized Christians', and maybe sell them cloth. Thirdly, America could supply England with raw materials like **timber** and furs. Fourthly, bigger ships would be needed for Atlantic voyages, and these could be used to defend England in emergencies.

Sir Walter Raleigh (c.1552–1618) – a writer, soldier, sailor and **courtier** – decided to put these ideas into action. In 1585, England and Spain finally went to war (see page 11). That year he found enough **backers**, including Queen Elizabeth I, to start a colony. He sent 600 men – about half of them soldiers – across the Atlantic to Roanoke Island. Roanoke is just off the coast of modern North Carolina in the USA.

Walter Raleigh was from Devon like Francis Drake. Tall, bold and good-looking, he was a favourite of Queen Elizabeth I.

Food shortages and fighting

Raleigh's colony was called 'Virginia' – after England's own unmarried 'Virgin Queen'. By August 1585, only about 100 colonists were still there. The rest had returned home after an accident on the dangerous coast, when sea water ruined much of the vital food supply brought out from England.

An experienced soldier, Ralph Lane, was in charge. Under his command, the men built a fort as a **privateering** base. Meanwhile the scientist Thomas Harriot made very full notes on the land and people, and artist John White drew detailed pictures.

During the harsh winter, before the colonists could grow their own crops, there was trouble. At first the Native Americans traded food for things like dolls and knives. Then the colonists started taking what they wanted by force. In one clash, the Native American chief was killed. Many of the colonists – weak, sick, hungry and disappointed – now wanted to abandon 'Virginia'. When Francis Drake visited Roanoke in June 1586, he agreed to take them home.

Raleigh's Roanoke project had failed. Or had it …?

A perfect place to settle?

Raleigh sent two captains, Philip Amadas and Arthur Barlow, to check out 'Virginia' in 1584. Their reports made it sound inviting – but they were trying to persuade others that a colony there could be successful: 'We found the people most gentle, loving and faithful ... They only wish to defend themselves from the cold in their short winter, and feed themselves with as much food as their soil gives them ... There are melons, walnuts, cucumbers, **gourds**, peas ... and their corn [maize], which is very white, fair, and well-flavoured.'

The City of Raleigh

In May 1587 Walter Raleigh sent a second group of **settlers** to Roanoke. Led by John White, they were **civilians**, not soldiers. There were even seventeen women and eleven children – including John White's own pregnant daughter with her husband. Walter Raleigh hoped the Native Americans would see that such a group wished only to live in peace with them. He announced that the **colony** would be called the City of Raleigh.

The men, women and children quickly set to work building a village. Their new wooden-framed homes must have looked quite like the Native Americans' huts (see picture). Food supplies were low, since on the voyage from England they had picked up little fresh food. They planted crops, and stocked up on local berries, oysters and other shellfish. As they settled in, some Native Americans – remembering the trouble two years before – watched with suspicion. Then, once again, trouble broke out.

Could the new colony survive?

The Native Americans belonged to different tribes. Some welcomed the colonists but others feared and hated the newcomers (see box on page 39).

A 1585 watercolour picture by John White, showing the Native American village of Pomeiock. Thomas Harriot, another settler, wrote in 1588: 'Their towns are small … the largest we have seen have only 30 houses. The towns walls are made of tree-bark tied to stakes, or of upright poles fixed close together.'

A bad beginning

John White kept a diary of Walter Raleigh's second Roanoke project. This is what he wrote soon after the colonists arrived in 1587. It shows that some Native Americans were not welcoming:

'28 July: George Howe was killed by savages [John White's harsh word for the Native Americans] who came to Roanoke either to spy on us or to hunt. They found him wading in the water, alone, unarmed except for a small forked stick that he was catching crabs with. He was shot with sixteen arrows then killed with wooden swords. After this they beat his head to pieces.'

It was hard for the colonists to know whom to trust – and once they shot at a friendly group by mistake. They tried to make amends by **baptizing** an especially helpful Native American and calling him 'Lord Manteo'. There was another joyful **christening** after John White's daughter gave birth to a healthy baby girl.

Then in August 1587 the colonists pleaded with John White to return to England to fetch much needed supplies. He did as they wished, but could not find a ship to bring him back until August 1590. Not one of the colonists was there to greet him when he returned. Had they all been killed, or moved to a safer place, or even gone to live with Native American groups? John White never learned the answer, and the mystery has never been solved.

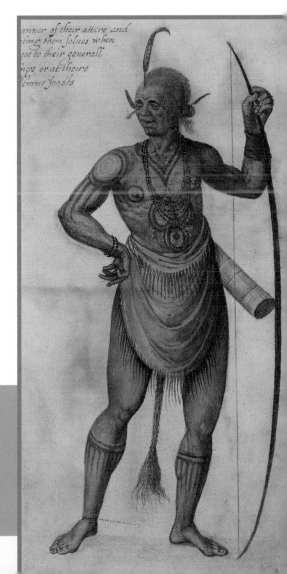

A Native American with his bow, painted by John White. Amadas and Barlow (see page 37) reported that 'their arrows are small canes, tipped with a sharp shell or the tooth of a fish.' The Native Americans also had wooden swords, wooden armour, and clubs with sharp animal horns attached to the end.

The quest for El Dorado

Spain's South American **empire** was rich in gold and silver. Yet Spanish explorers still travelled deep into the continent, looking for 'El Dorado'. Some rumours said this was a hidden city made entirely of gold. Others claimed it was a man, the ruler of a Native American empire, who dusted his body with gold each morning then simply washed it off at night. Either way, it sounded worth checking out.

By the 1590s, no one had found El Dorado. 'Experts' thought it lay in thick jungle up the river Orinoco, in the land of Guiana. In February 1595, four ships holding 300 men left England to investigate this further. The expedition's leader and organizer was Sir Walter Raleigh. He aimed to find a gold mine – which he believed to be the truth behind all the El Dorado stories. He also said he wished to 'save' the Native Americans from the cruel **Catholic** Spaniards.

The title page of Walter Raleigh's book about his 1595 exploration of Guiana. He made the land sound like a kind of paradise. The English, however, showed little interest in following up his expedition, and 'El Dorado' remained undiscovered forever.

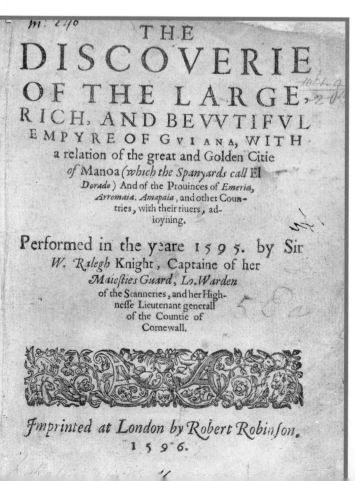

THE DISCOVERIE OF THE LARGE, RICH, AND BEVVTIFVL EMPYRE OF GVIANA, WITH a relation of the great and Golden Citie of Manoa (which the Spanyards call El Dorado) And of the Prouinces of *Emeria*, *Arromaia*, *Amapaia*, and other Countries, with their riuers, adioyning.

Performed in the yeare 1595. by Sir W. Ralegh Knight, Captaine of her Maiesties Guard, Lo. Warden of the Stanneries, and her Highnesse Lieutenant generall of the Countie of Cornewall.

Imprinted at London by Robert Robinson. 1596.

Tobacco mistaken as a health aid

Thomas Harriot (see page 37) took a great interest in smoking tobacco, a habit Europeans picked up from American Indians.

'You will see sailors and others who come back from America using little funnels, made of palm leaves or straw. In the end they stuff crumbled, dried leaves from the tobacco plant. This they light … and they suck in the smoke. They say this takes away hunger and thirst, restores strength and refreshes the spirit … This plant will be very valuable for curing sores, wounds, throat and chest infections, and plague fever.'

Thomas Harriot was possibly the first European man to die of cancer from smoking.

Fruits of the New World

Walter Raleigh's party set off up the river Orinoco in May 1595. For almost two months they mapped this unknown river, made records of the animals and plants they passed, and talked with the local people. However, they found no gold city, man or mine. With the crews suffering from tropical diseases as well as **scurvy**, they turned back. So ended the last great voyage of exploration during Tudor times.

Many explorers, like Sir Walter Raleigh, hoped to bring back precious or exotic goods from America. Some of them did; potatoes, turkeys and chocolate (from cocoa beans) were all quite new to Europeans. So was a 'new herb' much enjoyed by Raleigh himself – tobacco (see box).

Sir Walter Raleigh had one more try to bring back gold from Guiana, in the reign of the first **Stuart** king, James I. Again he failed, but by then a new North American **colony** had been started, at Jamestown in 1607. Unlike Raleigh's Roanoke projects, it succeeded. The English – already worldwide traders – would go on to settle in lands all over the globe.

How do we know? – *The Principal Navigations*

In 1607 some English trading ships were sailing to India. Near Sierra Leone, in West Africa, the fleet got into difficulties. The captain sent for 'the Book'. In it, he read a detailed description of the coast nearby, and so was able to find a safe place to shelter. By saving the ships and their **cargo** in this way, he saved his Company £20,000.

What was the valuable 'Book' he consulted? It was *The Principal Navigations, Voyages,* **Traffics** *and Discoveries of the English Nation,* written by Tudor priest Richard Hakluyt. First published in 1589, it was enlarged in 1598–1600 until it was 1,500,000 words long. When Tudor people usually spoke of 'the Book', they meant the Bible. For many seamen, explorers and **merchants**, the *Navigations* was just as precious.

A written record for all time

Richard Hakluyt first wrote down several of the stories you have read in this book. He spent years finding out about English voyages overseas. He researched ships' **logs**, merchants' reports, government papers and even papers captured from England's enemies. He also interviewed men who had taken part in some of the expeditions. No one paid him to do this. In fact he probably had to *pay* £50 – a huge sum then – to have his enlarged book published. Why did he do it?

Short versions of Richard Hakluyt's book are still in print today, over 400 years after he wrote it. Modern readers too can be inspired by his tales of heroic Tudor explorers.

Partly he wanted to pass on useful new information as the world became better known. Partly he loved knowledge for its own sake, and wished to share it with others. Partly he was so proud of the achievements of Tudor seamen that he wanted to celebrate them. We can still read his book today, and be amazed by the worldwide achievements of so many brave and skilful Tudor explorers.

This map from 1599, drawn by the mathematician Edward Wright, was included in the 1598–1600 version of Richard Hakluyt's *Principal Navigations*. 'You have here,' said the book, 'a true description of those parts of the world so far discovered.'

English people everywhere

During the reign of Queen Elizabeth I, Tudor merchants became busy all over the world. Richard Hakluyt proudly pointed this out in his book.

'Before our glorious Queen's reign,' he asked, 'who ever saw English merchants at Tripoli in Syria, Aleppo, Babylon and Balsara [all in the Middle East]? Who ever heard of Englishmen at Goa in India? And what English ships ever anchored in the mighty River Plate in South America … or traded with the princes of the Moluccas and the island of Java … or last of all returned home with rich **cargoes** from China?'

Timeline

1485	Tudor family begins to rule over England and Wales
1492	Christopher Columbus reaches America
1494	**Treaty** of Tordesillas divides up the world between Spanish and Portuguese
1497/1498	John Cabot's voyages to North America
1519	Spanish begin to build huge **empire** in America
1519–22	Ferdinand Magellan captains first expedition to sail around the world, but dies before voyage is complete
1529–1539	England stops being a Roman **Catholic** country
1555	Richard Chancellor's voyage to Russia
1557 & 1561	Anthony Jenkinson's journeys into central Asia
1576–78	Martin Frobisher's three voyages to find a north-west passage
1577–80	Francis Drake becomes first English sea-captain to sail around the world
1583	Humphrey Gilbert tries to start an American **colony**
1585–90	Walter Raleigh attempts to start English colony at Roanoke
1588	English navy beats invading Spanish fleet (or Armada)
1589	Richard Hakluyt publishes *Principal Navigations*
1595	Walter Raleigh attempts to find El Dorado in South America
1603	End of Tudor period

Sources and further reading

Sources

The author and Publishers gratefully acknowledge the publications from which sources in the book are drawn. In some cases the wording or sentence structure has been simplified to make the material appropriate for a school readership.

Big Chief Elizabeth – How England's Adventurers Gambled and Won the New World, Giles Milton (Hodder and Stoughton, 2000)

Elizabeth I and Her Reign, Ed. Richard Salter
(Macmillan Documents and Debates, 1988)

Elizabethan People, Ed. Joel Hurstfield and Alan G.R. Smith (Edward Arnold Documents of Modern History, 1972)

The Later Tudors, Penry Williams (Oxford, 1995)

The Queen's Conjuror – the Life and Magic of Dr Dee,
Benjamin Woolley (HarperCollins, 2001)

Sir Francis Drake – An Exhibition to Commemorate Francis Drake's Voyage around the World, 1577–1580, (British Library Board, 1977)

The Sixteenth Century, Patrick Collinson (Oxford, 2002)

Trade, Plunder and Settlement – Maritime Enterprise and the Genesis of the British Empire, 1480–1630, K.R. Andrews (Cambridge, 1984)

Tudor England, 1485–1603, Ed. Roger Lockyer and Dan O'Sullivan (Longman Sources and Opinions, 1993)

Further reading

John Cabot, Neil Champion (Heinemann Library, 2001)

Sir Francis Drake, Neil Champion (Heinemann Library, 2001)

Sir Walter Raleigh, Shaun McCarthy (Heinemann Library, 2002)

Exploration Overseas, Jane Shuter (Heinemann Library, 1996)

Tudor Explorers, Brian Williams (Heinemann Library, 1996)

Websites

www.heinemannexplore.co.uk – contains KS2 History modules including the Tudors.

www.brims.co.uk/tudors/ – information on Tudors for 7–10 year olds.

Glossary

ally close friend or supporter; it can be a person or a country

ambassador someone representing his king or queen abroad

apprentice young person learning a craft from a master

Arctic northernmost part of the earth

astrologer someone who studies the heavens to make predictions

backer someone who helps to pay for a project

baptizing going through a ceremony to become a member of a church

barge flat-bottomed boat

bilge water and rubbish that gathers in the bottom of a ship

breeches Tudor type of trousers

cable ship's rope

cargo goods carried by a ship

Catholic only Christian faith in western Europe until the 1520s, when people began to follow the Protestant faith

christening going through a ceremony to become a member of a church

civilians people who are not in the army or navy

cloves dried, scented flower-bud used to flavour food

colonies lands taken and ruled over by another country. The people who move there are known as colonists.

colonize to take over foreign lands and turn them into colonies

conquer to defeat completely in battle

courtier person who spent time at a monarch's court as a companion or adviser

cudgel blunt instrument used for fighting

empire collection of lands ruled over by a monarch

export to send goods out of the country to be sold abroad; or the name given to the goods that are sent

fevers illnesses with high temperatures

fined made to pay money as a punishment

flax blue-flowered plant grown for its fibres that can be woven

gourd large fleshy fruit of a climbing plant

horoscope predicting the future using date of birth

infidels term of abuse for people with a different faith

Inuits North American Arctic peoples, once known as Eskimos

log diary of a voyage

Low Countries old name describing the flat modern-day countries of the Netherlands, Belgium and Luxembourg

merchant person who buys and sells goods, to make money

monarch king, queen or other crowned ruler

mutiny rising up by the crew to take charge of a ship

naval to do with the navy

navigate directing a ship through its voyage

navigator person able to direct a ship throughout its voyage

neutral person or country that is not involved in a war

pilot experienced person who takes charge of a ship entering or leaving a harbour

Pope head of the Catholic church. He lives in Rome.

population number of people in a country

privateer person on a private ship allowed to seize enemy ships and goods during wartime. This was known as privateering.

profit money gained

Protestant religious faith of people who turned away from the teachings of the Catholic church

psalm holy song or hymn

Puritan Protestant who took religion very seriously

reef ridge of rock or coral below the water

rudder broad, flat wooden piece at back of ship used for steering

scurvy disease caused by lack of Vitamin C

settle to move to live in foreign lands or colonies

settlers people who move to live in foreign lands or colonies

shipwright man who designs and builds ships

spices strong-smelling vegetable products like pepper and cloves

strait narrow passage between two large stretches of water

Stuart name of the family that ruled over England and Wales after the Tudors

superstitious ready to believe in unknown or mysterious things

tax money paid by people to the monarch, to help pay for the running of the kingdom

timber wood used for making things

trade buying and selling of goods

traffics old-fashioned world for buying and selling goods

Treaty an agreement between two or more countries

Index